The Privacy *of* Wind

poems

PERIE LONGO

JOHN DANIEL AND COMPANY
SANTA BARBARA, 1997

ACKNOWLEDGEMENTS

"Even the birds could not believe…" published in *The Lucid Stone* (Summer 1995) and "Winter" published in *The Lucid Stone* (Winter 1995).

"Teepee at a Childhood Haunt" and "Morning After / Taking the Exam" published in *Prairie Schooner* (Summer 1995).

"The Privacy of Wind" published in *The Santa Barbara Independent* (December, 1992).

"The Writing Group" published in *The California State Poetry Quarterly* (Winter 1993).

My special thanks to my husband Phil and children Dana, Cecily and Paul for their love, support, and inspiration; to my sisters and brothers Nancy, Sue, Jim and Jerry for always being there; to poet friends Krishnaprema Jyothi, Lisa Meckel and Mary Sky Robinson for editing support and emotional sustenance; to Norene Wheeler for endurance; to the writing community of Santa Barbara and to all my students, who teach me what I most need to learn.

Printed in the United States of America

Published by John Daniel and Company
A division of Daniel and Daniel, Publishers, Inc.
Post Office Box 21922
Santa Barbara, CA 93121

Book design: Eric Larson

LIBRARY OF CONGRESS CATALOGING-IN-PUBLICATION DATA
Longo, Perie,(date)
The privacy of wind : poems / Perie Longo
p. cm.
ISBN 1-880284-23-5 (alk. paper)
I. Title
PS3562.O524P75 1997
811'.54—dc21 97-521
CIP

THE PRIVACY OF WIND

For my mother and daughter

Contents

Even the birds could not believe
the size of the loquats
like clusters of spun amber
at the top of the tree
above the neighbor's roof
where her eyes also reached
tracing the rush of wings
from the feeder in the strange
California June rain
She could tell by the way
they backed off
testing for an open space
to hook their feet

It was something for her
to believe again
in miracles of any sort
how you can almost create them
if you shrink the chatter
in your mind to a simple act of desire
like following the sound
of a drop

Litany

Anerca

Eskimo: to breathe, to make poetry

So let us begin. With trees.
Ones climbed to hide the catastrophe of having parents
when you're fourteen on a Sunday picnic at a lake,
your fingers juice stained from picking cherries
all come ripe at once on the fourth of July
and mother wants a pie for the tree to count
while you are happy to perch with birds in a crook
rescuing words. Let us remember trees that web sun
and you croon how the light throws down thin strings
to the center of your palm, and you grow warm sure your life
will never end no matter what the lines say.
We could go on with the lily-pilly dwarfed by the Queensland nut
in a grove just off the freeway behind a hospital where you wait
for news of one you love, when love was not enough
and muster hope in the gong of shade trees
that leave an ache deep in your neck as you search
for the spot of the song. Then there is the fire
where we left off last year, driving everything to the sea.
But trees.
Some stood charred in agony.
Just now some announce green to remind life is never lost.
Except on the surface. Cleaning delayed, in case a stray spark
should finish us off and I wouldn't want to spend my last months
this way, I have just now returned curtains to their rods
free at last from soot, just now placed the last painting
on fresh walls and marked photographs stored in a carton
for easy transport, "Sort!" No hurry. Ever.
This way for years, they hold us all together when the branching
gets out of hand. We must be ready to run backwards
and not hang ourselves on what has brought us this far.
Let us begin. Our poems. With breath.
The disillusion that brings us together. And triumph.
For we are eternal. Though surfaces tell us something else.
Let us begin with dark. And travel broad.

Lucy the Potter

How she loves the earth
become pulp she will shape
into her spirit too great to contain
the edge of an eagle's span and she will
shape the clay into a heart that has known
earth beneath earth soft later a vessel to hold
the heart like dough heart like rock heart never
tired at 90 heart that gets up even if she can't heart
that beats like wings ascending and when she has let
her spirit go from earth from stone she will walk away
clinging to the wing of herself design of mountains of
lightning strikes and they will know she has lived
the pot will call out for her over and over
no matter how large the dark grows
Come back come back
but she won't

A Time Before the Fall

My mother wants to see without glasses,
lays $3 down for a blouse
instead of $30. My sister says
put on your glasses. No she says
like no to each wrinkle, each line
no to each kindness, each reaching out
to catch her mind.
She does not want the present,
the snow, the sleet that bites her eyes,
what she sees, her children
older than she wants to be.
She wants her hair black again
to charm the men, wants to smell
magnolia and dip her feet
into white satin shoes
and spin herself dizzy
till she is six
safe in her beloved mother's arms.
Oh, she says, growing old
is no fun. You lose yourself,
then speaks of how she took the seniors' bus
to the store for the first time
since selling her car, how she could
find nothing she wanted
in the space of time. I didn't ask if
she wore her glasses. Perhaps the blur
is better, like how waterpaints blend
into such interesting bends with
just a little more water than called for.

Tepee at a Childhood Haunt

It was cold for summer and high and high and cold
though the close sun bragged of its summer strength
serving us like a gold host hot on the skin,
the Mosquito Range bold rising still further beyond
where I fished as a girl with my father on the banks
of the South Platte, him in water up to his knees,
me on my knees picking between ripples
for gems to line up on my window sill when home,
my heart a gourd, a rattle of seeds shaking with fantasy
to live on this earth some day, and in that crush of time
walking back to the car to carry me away from
the Native American Days, I saw it, the tepee
round and shining with the queerest light, as if cut
from electricity, pointed purposefully to the sun, poles
meeting at the center, the round that dizzies, brings us back
to the beginning as we open. Without thought I captured it
on film, maybe because there I was one with the earth
on my knees remembering smoke that spiraled in O's
that circled from my father's mouth and I would punch
my finger through them, to travel someplace my feet
could never go. Other times I followed his smoke
in the cold black night to the red glow like a siren
at the end of his cigarette, me staring at him long and cold
in the white night lit queer with the blink of danger.
One night he caught me like that, staring, a shadow
against his pain, an interruption in the cave where
he lived, a young girl fishing for some comfort against
his sadness and their fights, ugly words in the night like
fists against dough. My heart I thought would break, and
I grew afraid when he called my mother a name
not hers, froze hard and cold, fastened to his gaze.

In the photo of the tepee there is an interruption,
a streak of white smoke something like his spirit
passing across the heights as if pre-arranged.

Finally I am home satisfied, unfastened from the cold,
giving myself to earth, though my mother I am told
is white and lost, not herself, screams from across the country
she has been cheated, her eyes like the embers at the end
of my father's cigarette. Because she is right
in an old way, in an old way I enter the tepee
mounted on my wall, singular and clear, rising.

To My Mother Who Didn't Die After Her Fall As Predicted

How foolish of me
to say NO you will not die
when you almost did, foolish
to readily admit it must not have been time
just yet, ice clinging to the boughs outside
your long-term-care window. A halo
of white hair clings to your head that swelled
in your fall, shrunk memory
so you forgot everything that burned in you,
now you call everyone precious, your precious
jewels, even the nurse you barely know.

The last time we ever spoke,
you asked me over the phone
what am I to do now, now that they pay my bills.
My car is sold, what am I to do.
I sent you a set of watercolor pencils
and a pad of blank paper for your birthday,
but you have forgotten how to draw since the fall,
yet when I come again the next day, you ask for pencils
and paper. I fetch them from the car,
packed in a box to return home and save.
You pick out the colors you want, line them up
with a chant: white yellow blue green;
scrambled eggs potatoes peas coffee
and laugh making a joke on yourself.

I come a third day, my last to visit.
You show me your drawing I think to please
or appease me: a large white flower on white paper,
a shining center of yellow, the pine tree outside
your window, not the whole tree, just one side
where the ice has melted,
half a pine tree
a red splotch of color above
perhaps a cardinal praising the frost
and a sun there burning off my desire
to change the course of color or time,
though I am not ready for you to go,
your hand warm in mine.

Last I heard when I sent sister my love
to give you, you told her to tell me to stop
jumping on the bed.

sin

in the name of the father and son
the woman has lost herself at the sink
peeling potatoes, skins she reads
like tea leaves:
tomorrow you will take a long voyage
yesterday you lost your eyes
in the promise of security
today you feel stripped.

bless me father I do not believe in sin
I do not believe we commit ourselves
to darkness on purpose
we get mixed up
who is in us
and who outside pulls us off course.

don't leave when I say I love you
let it last longer than these few years
don't back away
after we have shared a story or two
don't punish me for not being you
I didn't mean to break the antique tea cup
on my way out the door
to my life
didn't mean to break apart a set, china
more precious than forgiveness
in those days

but now I am old and you are older.
now the snow is four inches deep you say
over the phone on Mother's Day,
over and over again *four inches.*
trouble four-hundred feet deep I say
and though your mind has drifted
to the outer rim
you say you are fine you are fine

like the china I think
as the snow blows cold on your end of the wire.
bless me mother as I tell you I am fine I am fine
I only wanted you to listen a long time ago
now there is nothing left to say
except goodbye then you chant
don't go don't go I don't want you to go.

I did not know those would be your last
words to me, did not know
I would sit by your side
three months later saying *I am here I am here*
I am sorry I am sorry for not talking
for not understanding what it was like for you
when I left so fast thirty years ago
without a backward glance, did not know
when you were saying all those other things

you were really saying don't go don't go
or please come please come.
I do not believe in sin, so set me a place
and I will bring the tea cup glued as it is
in the name of the father and son
and mother and daughter.

How Death Is

kept telling her you don't have to be afraid
kept saying she'd had a long good life
that dad would be there, her husband, her mother
waiting for her, kept saying how we wished
we could understand her after the stroke that took
her speech thoughts mind memory
but seemed to know us, her children her treasures
she called us her joy her life
tried to say our names it seemed her mouth moving around
some words the only one understood *please please please*
please what sweet dear please water please hold please up
please the tubes after all? please take you home
please don't let this happen I never thought it would
you so strong and sure of what was right
always there with your advice just comb your hair
put on a smile   a nice dress   tell him you love him
I love you always there with your talk, all your talk
all those words now only *please*
please let's dance let's laugh let's start all over go back
to the red brick house in Wauwatosa on 73rd Street
please don't suffer like this
please stay a little longer please go in peace
do you know I'm here   I thought you were
holding my hand but it is I who am holding yours
your hand pulling from mine floating off the white sheet
breathing with you sister and I at the end breathing with you
faster and faster, the labor so great, your diaphragm moving
up and down like a bellows to keep the lungs filling with air
but they are filling only with water more and more water
you are drowning in the last minutes the last breaths
we can't stop this return to the womb the vast womb
in this small compressed space   your breath rattle
louder and faster louder and faster and then

your face begins to blue   your breath slower
your face grows dark
and from you something swifts   I hear it go
watch it go
a sigh like a soft wind
and you are there no more
someone reached for you
I am small again
will have to cross the street alone
already you are talking   I feel it
your body just a pillow case on the bed
though you did not slip away   you powered off
like a lioness as you lived
I believe you were not afraid

White Winged Dove

At first I think the flick
in the bottlebush tree
outside my bedroom window
is a waft of morning air

but then I note that leaf is brown,
the others green,
and only one moves,
the shape a bit too long, the air
a bit too full of bounce

with a slash
of white as snow across
a ridge of spring mountains,
and lo! an eye, a round
of head. The body dull as smoke

and full, far larger than any perching bird
seems to beg for cuddling. I'm not sure
what bird it is.

From my quiet
comes the sound *mother?*
though she died 2000 miles away
more than a year ago. I am surprised,

move to the window
tell her to stay right there. I'll be out,
just stay, as if the dead would do anything
to please, give comfort
on a remote morning
with headlines full of bad news.

I am true to my word. Run
to the front door, slip
on the white hall tiles, stumble
past the juniper and abutalon, round
the corner and isn't that just like her,
this mother, this bird

there then not there,
a space in the dense tree
where she teased.

I shake my head like some young bird
in a child's book, head back to my work,
but not before checking reference.
A miracle! on the first page I turn to,

my mother's picture in profile
with a sharp gold eye:
White Winged Dove!
There's more if I turn

to page 510. I flip the leaves
and read: its cooing sounds like
who cooks for you-all. Of all
the questions she could ask!
When she comes again

I will not move.
I will sit still and reply
what she already knows,
this mother now of peace, *I do, I do.*

Of Sara Scuderi, Age 87, Listening to Herself Sing "Visi d'Arte" at 28

She enters a room almost bare, just a tall window,
a table, a chair, like an aged painting this room,
that would leave dust or splinters on your fingers
if you touched. The room is filled with something else
she knows but can hardly believe, her voice
clear, free of strain.
Is it really her? Her?
Then? Was it real then?
She places her gloved hand
on the back of the chair, slowly
sinks, her eyes looking for where the sound
is coming from after all these years
and then unable to contain her joy
she begins to hum along not for what she has lost
but what she hears again, feels
at every breath, the beauty
still hers no one sees. Her fingers begin to tap
the melody against her worn coat sleeve
as she whispers "beautiful,"
her eyes glistening "beautiful"
and she is, more now than ever, embossed
in time's frieze. The fine fox hairs
of her coat collar quiver on a high note.
You can almost see the sequins shimmer
on her breast, watch a cascade of dark hair
fall from beneath an old wool hat pressed down
on her head. And then the recording ends
in this bare room where she remains
and closes her eyes over herself.

Old One

What was that song
Those words that bled
Through my Mother
When great Father said it was
Time to go
When the deer fell under
The arrow of hunger

Quickly must I remember
Before my mind turns solid
As this drum I hold
Quickly must I remember
Before embers that fire my heart
Fade

All my children are gone
Far too fast with the force
Life wills upon us
May this song I remember
Protect them from the cold that
Falls over my shoulders

On the mountains woven
Into the shawl I wear
To warm these old bones
Becoming soft
Like my thoughts that dip
And rise to the light

From the fire singing
In a land I can almost see
With no vision
My heart beating against walls
That no longer contain
My need

Litany

Our Lady of the Waterfall   lead us to high cliffs
    that we may feel   our spilling over
Our Lady of Mistaken Identity   help us find ourselves
Our Lady of Elephants   lift us from our weightiness
        gracefully
Our Lady of the White Blossom which repeats itself
    over and over again   April after April
        pray for us
Our Lady of the Red Fox   running for its life
        across a busy street
        have mercy on us
Our Lady of Politics   pray for the lessening
        of stupidity from the bullheaded
Our Lady of the Post Office   we pray for no more junk mail
    on how to avoid aging or high cholesterol
Our Lady of Old Age   pray we grow as the mountain
        which may also suffer osteoporosis
Our Lady of Persuasion   relieve us from judges,
    truth-twisting defense attorneys, criminals who
        get away with murder and named politicians
        as they slink through shallow waters
Our Lady of Sharks   pray for our avoidance
        of things that go bite in the dark
Our Lady of Perpetual Commotion   pray for our stillness
Our Lady of Tomatoes   pray that mine recover
        from underwatering, overwatering,
        bugs, snails, and my cat who bats their tendrils
Our Lady of the Theatre   may life have a starring role
Our Lady of Duty   pray for us to step from
        the necessary to the essential
Our Lady of Safety   restore the innocence of children
Our Lady of the Soul   lead us to the white space
        that fills the world
    with all who came before   and will after

Between Heaven and Hell

Winter

As a child I didn't know what kept snow away
from our house or how a crocus could poke a ring
through ice, but I knew frost could tell about dreams
of ferns in the woods and that Judy R. pointed
her finger laughing at me not because I wore
brown ugly hightop shoes to correct crooked feet
but because she was afraid of what I wrote at recess,
leaning against the wire fence that kept the ball
from rolling out and the world from crashing in—
or so the teachers thought, not knowing children
mimic all the slaughter, and they just couldn't see
the damage done during history class, but I showed her,
that Judy, I climbed the highest mountain in the USA
with straightened feet and I bet she never knew
the sky weighs nothing on your back
and that her mocking didn't quiet me too long
maybe because my sister said never mind
the day she wrapped her plaid wool scarf
around my neck before I took off in the cold
to find out how different snowflakes were from each other
and why they lost their shape, shoveled aside
to make a path to the dairy two blocks away
where we trudged for milk at dawn before plows came,
made a path into a day that would never repeat itself
until now and that a moment could come again and again
for the rest of your life like how the black
seeds of a watermelon always hold the green.

CORDUROY

The first time I tried to say corduroy, the fabric
of my favorite dress, my lips could not break out
of their O to glide to the R which escaped me
completely as if my mouth was a spoiled instrument.
So cute, the way she cannot talk, they said.
The first time my mouth moved around corduroy
I had practiced for years in front of the mirror,
in disguise of a tiger roaring
or any other R word I could get my mind on—
then splitting the sounds—cord cord, erase
erase, roooy, brrrr in Wisconsin winter frost.
The first time I said corduroy I raced
to my girlfriend's down the street
who had no idea why I should care I could say
green corduroy dress
as she sat in her black velvet robe.
I felt more beautiful than Mary H.,
the most beautiful girl in the school who always
played the romantic leads in the plays
while I would take less fortunate roles like beasts
who could finally roar.
    "How are you today," Mary asked.
    "Corduroy," I replied.
    "You're an odd one," she'd snicker.
"Brrrr," I trilled racing down
the locker-lined hallway, "I am corduroy.
I am ribbed. I am whaled. I am spouted.
I have arrived. I am not ashamed of my mouth.
I have grown up. I will play the lead.
I can say anything I want." I could, at least
until love came along, far harder than corduroy.
And all those words and phrases that followed,
the roars and crashes. Triumphs and defeats.
I am still practicing in the mirror, trying
to get how I love you, right.

Skip to My Lou

What am I supposed to do on the feet
of a last refrain? Run to kneel,
beg for understanding? Mercy I
could not make my words passed

from hand to hand reach the confines
of your mind shrunk moon thin behind
turns of razor-sharp wire in the soft
washed night? What sung images

could make you full again? Free again?
make you trust I will not leave
because I love you, only because
you leave me no other choice,

and soon as I ask I know, nothing.
A poem cannot save the day
or walk you into sun so I will not
try to reach you again. What is a poet

to do who learns words so discreetly picked
have been set to match, sacrificed to air
you breathe unconsciously. Generations
of trees sifted through cracks in my house

last year and drawing my hand across
the tintype of a great-grandmother
to remove their remains I saw
how I had come to resemble her.

I will not show this hand to you again
but should our gaze fasten
some future round, should my heart skip
I will hold that space for our escape.

Marching Flamingos at the Nassau Zoo

Even the minister of affairs was impressed
Amos said when twenty years ago
he commanded the flamingos "advance"
with a snap of his switch, as now
and they gather in rows
like uncooperative cobs
then amble spindily forward
not exactly marching as advertised,
rather they run as an unparalleled wave
of insecure pink not sure where to break;

not exactly in unison, more in delirium,
their unblinking eyes blazoned
on the sprinkle of audience ordered
to applaud to keep them performing.
Though my daughter and I prefer to be bobbing
in tropical waters today churned beyond reason
in a freak storm,
we are making the best of it, enjoying
this stumble into historical compliance,

so as one flamingo fails to about his face
catching sight of a single black swan
snuck under the barricade
wanting nothing more than to finally belong,
never mind his color, his squatness,
the out of sync army of pink skitters
one way, while this single flamingo
glances over the flanks, spreads his wings
in the jungle of complacence,
brave not by will, daring not by gall,
and flaps backwards in objection
while we forget our orders and laugh.

"Get on now," Amos switches, "retreat,"
and for one moment we all revel in the reverse,
the obstinance, the delight that a flock in hand
is no flock at all,
the swan aside in the straw
craning its long neck after Amos' switch
he would be glad to follow
given the chance, unsure
what the rush is about
finally arrived in the wake.

The Passion Vine

I do not know how I have come to this place
of my life, unable to resurrect a metaphor
to name the shaking or loss,
no word to hold the emptiness
or make it something else.

Last night I left the house
to find this word, walking around a neighborhood
so familiar I could tell you each tree or plant that grew
around each house, who had just weeded,
or who was out of town by the way the curtains hung,
and there in the mood of no moon,
became lost as if I had never seen the intersection
where I stood, street signs just pieces of green tin,
white letters like splotches of hurried paint.

In sleep, again
no dream remembered, sun
risen early, time fallen back to give us
more light in its waning. I went out to check
the garden as I always do at dawn, and thought
too much purple, all the gold influence fallen like light
in the turn of season, freshly planted broccoli
and brussel sprouts beginning to plump
but then I was faced with my rashness, the passion vine
I so loved and nurtured for months, trained
to wind and climb in this or that direction,
hacked off at its base the day the caterpillars
triumphed and I could not forgive
myself for letting them
have it.

At first I was kind
when the caterpillars appeared,
but when an inch becomes a map of a whole country
I snap
          and so it was with the caterpillars
I thought would nibble only a few leaves
here and there, leaving the white passion flowers
as invitation to long glance.

Oh yes I was kind
carrying them safely in a sterile mayonnaise jar
with holes poked in the lid for safe ride to the nursery.
When I asked how to get rid of them
without toxicity, the woman who I questioned
laughed, I was a funny one
wanting both things at once.
     You must choose, she said.
So I released them to the field to eat something else
and not come back or they'd be sorry.

When I found every leaf of the vine chewed ragged
days later, so only the skeleton remained,
a long brown bone with the caterpillars
riding the stalks like children on a rollercoaster
screaming in joy, I carefully picked the white flowers
matured to orange fruit hanging sadly
like ornaments on a dead Christmas tree,
     then tore the vine madly from the railing,
not kindly, and cried as when each child
I grew left home for this or that reason

but now here is this tendril
I lift and wrap around a post   as far as it will go.

To my Daughter on Her 8th Grade Graduation

Have I told you how your face reflects
something translucent, whirl of light
as pearl cradled inside abalone, tears
not wept? This pull I feel rows away
as you sit with awards limp on your lap,
your shoulders drooped over black polka dots,
eyes brimmed with something desired,
deserved, something they could not give you,
not knowing how to name it,
as a teacher said, an honor not invented.

Have I told you how everything fits together
sooner or later, sorrow slipping over ecstasy
as the sea fades into sky on silver days,
and just so what burns inside
will ease you into the dream of yourself,
the sky full again with wings,
your life as it is and by the way thank you
for coming into mine,

for rolling toward me on skates down
the same street I used to stroll you,
yesterday your hands filled with spare flowers
that managed to sing in the drought,
jacaranda, marigold, mayflower and a small
purple stalk I cannot name so delicate
and sure of itself in the glass
on the table where we take the comfort of tea
and plan the summer ahead.

Have I told you I would cry for you
if I could, but then how would you know
the other side? And would you notice the flowers?

Lunch Break

A ridge of jacaranda profuse
above brick walls barely disguises
an obnoxious rise of rooms and winding halls
that have digested my daughter and spit me out
into the courtyard since the print out of her heart
showed it could no longer endure on its own,
not weak of its own accord but diminished
for return to days full of cartoon birds,
rainbows, a grinning sun with dark glasses
and a mother who could do no wrong.

Today I no longer need the whole
outdoors. Only a finch seeking crumb
is enough, this mantle of shade
from rusty leaf fig beginning to form.
I must learn to settle on pieces and strips,
half words. Nibbles. An ant speeding
on shed leaf. The movement of her heart
not unlike the charting of whale song.
Groans. Clicks. Her expression
a dirge or decompression. The space
between murmurs of her pulse
the language of grief, a cave from which
no one enters or exists. Eating lunch

I no longer mind the jet, the siren,
the jam of smasher into concrete.
One more bite of bread. In a few beats
I will see her again, will hold her close
to my heart which is not enough,
which gets in the way
and tell her about this feeding.

Eating Plums

For a month you have been gone
from home, your thin shell of body
unable to support shadows in a mind
traveled too far beyond itself.
It is no use, this loss. And now
the staff of experts removes me
in their antiseptic gaze as we visit
behind locked doors in the dining room,
the only place I am allowed, where
we sit at dusk thrilling over ripe plums
I picked from a neighbor's tree,
juice running down our chins
onto the plastic orange table
where you are a prisoner at mealtime,
every calorie you ingest counted
to assure you gain the weight to make
you strong again. I am more
than grateful for this intervention
especially to see you doing this,
eating this plum, enjoying the mess
of nourishment just this minute
unafraid you will take up more space
than you deserve. I cannot describe
the pleasure of this juice all over us
with no towel around to wipe us clean
as you break through the skin
of your plum, sink teeth
into its umber sweetness drawn
from dry ground. Now I can leave
on the river of your smile, the seed
of what we once were in hand.

In the Wings

She wants to hear herself sing
sing a high note carry it off
to where trees don't even grow
so somehow it will strike havoc
with a goddess roaming out there
wherever goddesses go and come
back down to earth
this sad tired wet yes finally earth
and turn a trick or two in the middle
of her black hole opening its mouth
and all the time she thought
it was only some possibility
light years away so there she is
wanting to hear herself sing
and some grizzled black fur creature
with red eyes comes by
takes her voice says no you can't have it
it's mine I'm bigger than you
and she goes off for the life
of a fairy tale crying if you listen
waiting for that control
a purposefully molded sound
angry high and sure
when it comes she will know
there will be a new sun new life and
she yes who waits will have back
what they took
how her song will rise

Between Heaven and Hell

"It's such a bore—it means I shall have to
turn you out—which I absolutely loathe…"
—Olive in *Ways and Means* by Noel Coward

between the ocean and concrete wall of the theatre
i repeat my lines over & over as if i could get them right,
as if i could give each syllable some nuance to make my appearance
meaningful, as if the night would make a difference
if i delivered my words with the proper finesse
of a British aristocrat when in truth I am a woman of caves
as if my tears hidden behind false irises could mean anything
but something to catch the light. no, here i am only one
of the puppets, as the reviewers say, a part i learned early
and quickly as earth is puppet to sun, leaf to tree. mother
to daughter to mother. don't we all dangle between heaven & hell
any day of the week. don't we all spend our lives as highlight
to something darker, support of something weaker, we women,
we mothers who bow and bow begging for our lives to turn out
like some slick meal no one wants,
our daughters aching to take their places, afraid they'll confuse
others' lives as we did theirs trying to dance on someone else's string.
how i tried to turn her out whole, coming through me as she did,
yet each day she sheds more and more of her glorious self
as i reach out to raise her up, ask for another chance,
change anyway possible as i clutch limp flowers for the ghosts
of what could have been, and

dangle
tangledasiam pretending to be fine and refined, turning
in the twilight to the crow's taunt, my clown red mouth
screaming down god *why her why her* with no rehearsal,
perfect inflection no one will ever hear.

When You Were Born

Dare I speak of my fear you may die,
how you blur on the other side
of some electric chain-link fence,
how I am reaching out to keep you intact
any way I can so in your absence
something will have definition to our lives
besides this picture, the shape of your face
I trace with my finger each morning, each time
I pass into my office, trace as the morning
you were born, your whole small face nested
in my hand not believing the miracle of you,
your eyes more deep than any forest and filled
with great swiftness as if you rushed to me
without thinking and changed your mind.
Don't think I haven't thought of it,
how you would have been better off
with another mother, someone more staid,
more spunky, less spunky, more frivolous,
less serious, less poetic, more scientific. Now
that you have taught me how to grieve,
hold myself in your loss, I wonder with my heart
ground to powder if there is anything I have
given you, can give you—to carry you where
you need to go that is no business of mine.

Just after your seventh birthday
you came from play saying Wonderland
had disappeared. It will return, you know.
I saw it in your gaze when you were born.
Someday you will look in the mirror
and it will be there again. It may be only a flash.

I stand at the pay phone in the hall of one hospital
talking to another hospital, again, as you pack your things
in shopping bags preparing to fly, no suitcase on hand in the flurry.

Yesterday they agreed to treat you. Now they have changed
their minds. Again. You can come, you can't, you can, you can't,
our insurance refuses to pay. I am taffy on the line. You live,

you live not, you live, live not.
                                        No room at the inn.
Survival of the fittest rings in my ears along with Jingle Bells,

time running out. I remind them of commitment,
of duty and suddenly they weaken *come then* (all ye hopeful)
                                        and before they revert we are
                                        in the car up the freeway to the airport,

maneuvering through slow traffic *just like in the movies*
I tell you, screeching into the parking lot no minute to spare,
the departure gate too far away, you too weak, shaking too hard.

I cannot carry it all, you can barely walk.
Think strong I beg *this time you must promise me.*
People stare as we struggle, stare and turn away, trip on our things

that spill from the bags. But I have harkened others
who join us, grandmothers and grandfathers,
aunts uncles friends, all those who have gone before, and then we are air
                                                  borne and breathe,

drink water and breathe
we have made it this far, then we are landing, in a taxi, at the motel
because we cannot check into the hospital until next morning
and then we have to eat. You think you can, I know
you must. But first we cannot resist Christmas at the mall,
the colored lights, the push, the caroling and in this strange place

we buy each other hats, red plaid jaunty hats,
pose before a mirror smiling, mother and daughter
crowning each other queens for the night. And we never
                                        take them off, not even next day
                                        when they say they've made a mistake,
we'll have to leave but I say we deserve a chance after
all this. You tell them how your grandmother died exactly one year
ago down the hall, dare suggest yourself an opportunity not unlike

the Infant himself. They look askance, these not very wise men,
take your vital signs, test your heart, rush you to the cardiac ward,
hook you to machines and IV's in your red plaid hat.

When your father blows in Christmas eve, red-cheeked,
we celebrate the only way we can, sing not very silent, and
                                        read the old sustaining story

in this white, cold room, stars outside the window on fire,
green teeth of the heart monitor dipping and rising
intermittent bleeps background to the harking angels not so high.

Sound of Arroyo Burro Creek During a Once-in-a-Lifetime Rainstorm

All the water held above like years of denial
come down at once, the backyard filling, roof leaking,
hills sliding, fifteen feet of runoff under
the downtown overpass, warriors with no war
to fight jumping in, we come to check the banks
of the creek, if they can endure such dumping.
I have never heard such a symphony of rage
as the back of the creek explodes into muddy arc
through a four-foot pipe, this same pipe once a cave
for my child who ran here when afraid,
who sang here and lifted from her body on the echo
of her voice, who loved me so much
she would even share this great secret with me
before leaving one summer, the day
our paths split. And the sound my heart made
is here, its groan holding what is hardly bearable,
banks caving in, clay gone to ooze, water a hide
of brown tepees, sound of buffalo on the rampage,
the creek a war cry of water spreading to meet
more and more creeks jumped their beds
run away from home like our children
who can't take the limits anymore. Later I drive
to the ocean which leaps with joy at the feast,
swallows all the overflow whole, absorbs
what we cannot control. On my knees
to photograph how land and sea are one,
this one day in who knows how many centuries,
there is a voice, a sweet lilt calling *mom* surfing
the crest of all that commotion. *I thought I'd find you*
here, she says. *I thought the same* I say and
take her picture too, where everything meets.

The Privacy of Wind

Poet This Side of the Fire

Shortly after she had a stroke shortly after her husband
walked out, a woman stuttered over the phone, shortly after
she wrote a poem, sent it in for a contest, now had won
a gold medal, been invited to read it in Las Vegas, was it a scam
as friends warned, I'd been referred. Worried about the gusts
and heat, what to assemble for dinner and what to say to poets
next day at the conference, some wanting to be heard
more than anything, wanting their pain to have a grave,

others hoping to find their voices safely bedded between
the sheets of a perfect phrase, I asked did the prize
include the trip and that was the problem, she won nothing,
would have to pay $495 but that included two days
and a night of fame, an audience of 4000, Bob Hope for laughs,
other movie stars and oh yes a banquet with champagne,
excuse her intrusion, but yesterday she was nobody.
Today a poet not knowing where to turn. I told her,
the sky gone smokey, it's just money and wished her luck.

The fire moved quickly down canyon through town,
one woman found burned, her portrait printed in the news,
her eyes whole and haunting and I ask what to do, spared,
the fire satisfied just short of our street. When a friend
offered for my holding remains from her mother's home,
a grandmother's engraved mirror, and a pottery bell
in the shape of a cow, I felt a lowing that will not cease,

all that wildness downed to a hollow of gray,
bowls and bowls of gray and wonder if the fire spoke
for all those who never had an audience till now
as we drive past chimneys, pick through char searching
for some object, some body to tell us how to save ourselves
no matter what the cost this side of the mountains
where sundowners blow when it gets too hot and lonely,
the sea beyond still blue for laughs, the sky whole and there.

What Price Rock

We've done it. Torn up the lawn
impatient for rain. Planted it with sticky things
whose names I don't have time to pronounce
like *Helianthemum numularium*
and *Perovskia abrotanoides* which sound like aberrations
to me, or incurable diseases. No wonder Rome fell
fending off an attack from behind a wall
of *Artemesia arborescens.*

Give me a break, I tell our horticultural consultant.
He translates one for a price, "Breath of Heaven."
I can get into that, fingering
heaven's greenish-gray fronds whispering
love me love me in an Indian breeze
above bark spread to hide despicable drip hoses.

Don't get me wrong. I'm happy
to do what I can to preserve dribbles,
it's just I need to highlight the twigs I'm promised
will grow four feet tall in two years or more,
and then I remember seeing huge rugged rocks
in the botanical garden, shaped like warrior masks
and gnomes and seals on the beach,
rocks age has painted with Rorschach designs
on a second skin, and I want two
or three or more or more.

20 cents a pound, she says,
from McNall's. They come by crane.
By crane, I echo like an innocent
dreaming of a rock tied in a white cloth
hanging from the beak of a stork,
a rock I will stroke and feed poems,
burp if it needs and graze on waiting for rain.

Wild with hope I rush to the masonry,
choose three lichen-adorned
interestingly twisted boulders, surely destined
to bask in my brittle garden, 1200 pounds of rock.
Because I am so thrilled
they willingly give me a deal,
only $900 total cash on delivery
set in stone. I think of my grandmother
thirty years ago shopping for a gravemarker

who said she couldn't afford to die
when she heard the price,
and she didn't and to this day
we say oh grandma, she's just out
in the garden behind the rain
and me I'm doing the same, testing
which small rocks we carried down
from the mountain look best where
warming up to *Zauschneria* and *Miscanthus.*

Now each time I pass a boulder hiking up
some trail I sing you jewel, you jewel!
You highlight of resistance! You strength
of sorry spirit! You erosion of my bank account!
What price your granite be,
while the Breath of Heaven sends forth
its fragrance rising to the occasion.

Getting It Straight

for Krishnaprema

It's true the plants around our house are dying
except a few fed with tea water,
that keeping much more alive than a bush or two
and ourselves, is more than we can handle.
Our arms like wings for balance, we cross
the plank over the turtle pond gone dry
like so much else these days. We hope the turtles
have found another place to swim as we seek
a way to keep our heads above water
when there is none around.

It's true we're getting older
and will not rinse our hair blue
no matter how unevenly grey it grows,
or unbalanced we become, because any head above water
is worth two below, and did you hear a man
with a brain tumor wants to freeze his head
until they discover a cure for cancer,
however long it takes so that he can attach it
to another body when the time comes. I wonder

if he will tremble when he wakes up on another plane
with no one around to understand how it was
before. I've seen this happen. To rats, long ago
when I helped my father transplant the brain of one
to another and when the chosen one revived
from surgery it never responded to its name
or my singing and lived out its days waiting
for something that never came.

If my father were alive it's true
he might be called to task for animal cruelty
but he would say he was only trying to discover
ways to stretch life back into itself
and he might cry, as when his father died,
and when I saw he was beyond my comfort,
understood what he meant finally when he said
if one person understands you,
you will never want more. Yes we will try

to tend our children while we have the chance,
and let ourselves cry when they leave home
to seek new ground to call their own
while we wait nervously chewing our nails
instead of polishing them and pray gratefully
our homes did not burn in the fire
that galloped right up to the doorstep
as if to warn us any sweeping could be a lesson
in futility when nature sets its course.

So as petroglyphs inside the dark
Chumash cave fenced against vandals,
circle bright against our gaze, I think
what we create for ourselves may come to nothing,
may not be understood or misinterpreted,
ground for disrespect or posterity,
or something else, and all this to confess
I'm hoping you will write poems again,
and when the rains come we will not wash away
before putting our feet down
and getting it straight.

The Privacy of Wind

Once I read when you find yourself accidentally
on top of the mountain
and come down, you can never be there again
without struggle, namely in service of others, though
I was not thinking of this last week pressing up
against the wind, the privacy of wind that insisted itself
upon me despite my wish for only pleasure,
to feel the machine of the body that overrides routine.

In the beginning I lost my breath
so excited to be rising again, but it came back quickly
as I moved into the thinness
of high blue, adding layers as I went,
two shirts, sweater, scarf around my ears,
over that a sun visor and #25 on my nose,
youngsters running up and down in swim suits
as if they were breath itself. Only when
the trees ran out did I realize why I forgot
pen and paper this trip, for wind

to have its way and I would be old enough to hear.
It was then the music of lonely earth swelled
beneath and I could not stop
except to photograph the mildest wildflower
nestled in a grotto of volcanic rocks
or pick my way through snow that had no grip
in summer when the mountain opens its gates
not in kindness but bears our intrusion
only to behold something besides white
and one flower. When finally there was no place

to go but over the edge, I remained steady
in the wind, the privacy of wind,
rolls of excess rises far below. And while thinking
we don't have as long to spend as nature
repairing ourselves after eruptions
and how long it would take to silence
the white of my mind, a woman approached.
Did I have an extra film. Her husband, stupid ass,
had messed up the camera. Well maybe it wasn't
his fault but she had to get mad at someone.

I told her 75 years ago the mountain exploded,
she was walking on its tears large as they were.
But she didn't hear in the wind
so I met her where she was, offered my camera,
would send her the prints. This was no help.
They had to be there in the picture
or who would know or believe. To climb
all this way was pointless, was nothing
without proof. All I could do was look out

past the caldera down at the lake
like a blue eye winking and felt the mountain
moan I swear. You will know
I whispered, but she didn't hear
in the wind which near took off her hair.
Would I mind possibly could I snap them over near the rim,
with Mt. Shasta over their shoulder
to give perspective. Of course yes
and of course I did. That was just the beginning. Soon
she had other ideas, one with the snow field in back,
how about here. And there. And there like a child
she skipped, her daughter just grinning,
her husband squinting so close to the sun.

Where was I from, she asked, as if we should be friends
since I was performing this service,
and when it was the same town where her first husband
was from, she ran out of shot, uncontained
with shock at proof of the world's smallness
even here. Did I know him, a store front boasted his name,
her claim to fame she blushed. Well now you have another
I said, considering where she stood
and she stopped short. Him? pointing to the stupid ass
who looked quite proud and

I caught them like that
with nothing of importance behind in the privacy of wind.

The Scream

Up there on the mountain I learned,
with my leg a Z on the snow, that pain
is hot and cold at once, that it can pull noises
from you you only thought could come from
train whistles in Siberia.
The ski patrol warned me it would hurt
when he put my leg in traction, that I could scream.
So when he gave my leg a long steady pull,
as if it was being stretched across the continental divide,
gears that had never budged
unclogged and there it was, this scream,
not like a Siberian train whistle after all,
more like every nightmare coiled together rolling
across the mountain, maybe creating avalanches
to free more aches than mine, than hers, than ours.

All thoughts cease in this deep freeze place
a week later home in bed. Forty staples
pull at the seam where they inserted the rod.
Maybe this accident is about feeling
what has held me together besides skin,
for instance all of us stumbling and rising again
like spring. Up there inside the mountain's heart,
I didn't know the sky could be so blue or wide,
and I couldn't say I love you loud enough
out of focus as I was, wrapped like a mummy
in plastic, one with snow's slickness, the scraping
metal of the toboggan an illusion of strength.
I didn't know a scream could feel so good,
could straighten a leg, could bring the sun down,
could end a war.

Ode to a Broken Bone

Oh femur of mercurial mood,
Oh muscles of monumental fatigue
and indefatigable feats like how you once
assisted me to navigate mountains and meadows and seas,
I beg you to repair sooner than soon.
No gold or bronze or silver medals to praise
our massive triple axle twist accomplished
tripping on the slush of a run
unkindly named AXE HANDLE!
dear bone, and you shattered like a piece of china on tile.
What if I were to spend the rest of my life
perched on crutches like a flamingo,
my good leg firm and strong,
you fluttering like a loose rail
    on an old clapboard fence in an abandoned town
        in the wind on an empty road.

I admit I don't feel quite so alone
now I read the pope broke this very same bone
just last week! Oh careless doctrine,
oh unorthodox transgression! Forgive me
but truly you are a pain in the bottom I have hit.
I am listening, waiting for the answer
to the question greater athletes than I
have asked—"Why me? Why me?"
                the only reply mustered like a ghost
                                "Why not?   why not?"

Unable to budge out of the pathless woods of my brain,
I praise your future swing, wired as you are to a metal rod,
and ride your lessons humbly. Perhaps in this rest,
oh leg of mine, oh femur, I will appreciate
where we have been, what we have done
and undone, gone too far.

Learning to Walk

Starts with sitting still, listening
to how time lengthens in silence.
A friend moves off the horizon, her words
of comfort a hook to grasp, to cling to
like the steel traps I sometimes throw down
in disgust. Need greater than pain, I pull myself
to the counter, reach for the cup,
the coffee, the spoon, inch it like a worm
from sink to microwave. Brew.
Place the cup on a chair, push it across
the floor with my good leg scrape by scrape
back to the table, collapse, drink.
Watch the purple delphinium petals drop
and not make a sound, not try to get up again,
knowing their bloom is over. We forget
the softness and light when a child cries
at the life provided and tear our hearts apart
a million times over, looking for the reason
as illusive as why anything happens.
Why apples are green or wheels round.
Why we lose attention, forget we're on a downhill
ride with all the pushing up,
so I push against the stiffness as I sit,
do what I am told to build up my quads, slide
my rabbit soft footed sock back and forth
across the slick tile floor flatter than snow,
push the blade of my will
across all the small and grand favors.
And when a pin drops casting a fine note that echoes
in the empty house I know I must retrieve it,
no matter how far I have to reach, must go
out of my way, for going forward, for good luck.

Morning After Taking the Exam

What is a singed wing to a soul made firm
in its failing.
What do you think eternity is all about
though interest is beyond you at the moment
                                        right-angled to a stream
of traffic locked intent on penetrating
the freeway and you think all that matters
is that some empathic heart
will let you in,
                                                        break entrance
into a chain going no where
anyway.

What is this wrong turn
to the exquisite caress of a friend's piney voice,
how it becomes a symphony against the odds.

Think of the bristlecone pine your mind bonded with
last summer high in the White Mountains,
its bark made impenetrable to bugs
with the whipping of 200 mph winds day after day,
blizzards that drive off any breathing thing
yet in the short span of summer heat
how it expands enough to know
the transiency of flesh,
its twisted self seeking not shelter   but solace
soft to your leaning,
another microscopic ring added to its 4000 plus,
just another wrinkle for you,
this test, this blizzard of words that add up to
no thing
as if four choices were all we had anyway
only one correct.

Come now

you are safe within the fire.
What are you but a flame.
What is anyone but fuel. The jam is still jammed
and you have reversed yourself down a road
lined with trees between flower groves.
An oboe riding deep on air wave recesses grows
in such abandon, returns you to your core, a choice
they never thought of
not a word spoken. A little wind
Let them know you passed.

Girl i Say

even though my flesh these days acts like
it just wants to get down, lounge around
doing nothing. Girl, get going
move those bones off the patio
your eyes off those butterflies come flitting
off the far fields two by two.
Straighten those cupboards, line up those papers,
package those thoughts, have that party, girl
what's stopping you?
Girl, i say, your mama did the best she could
with her southern ways in a western world,
with a fishing flower growing mind-wandering
mountain-loving man.
Now you're sea level
there's always a hurricane just waiting
on the other side of a train's jangle
reminding you of those Gypsies on the plains
with no place in mind to travel, just to travel.
It's going down the road that matters, girl
going till it dips
like yesterday when you stood on top
of a water slide
like a bear cresting the mountain
yelling not this way, it's switchbacks
and earth i'm used to, going slow,
all those words rushing you over the edge
and you screamed eyes covered all the way back
with a splash about whale size into all those days lived
back to the beginning,
feet first.
Girl, you get to start again each day
so you might as well take that thumb out of your mouth
and live it,
like your mom and daddy taught you, up.

The Price of Evolution

yes will you look
at that tendril reaching out
for something to help it climb, how it twines around
itself
until there is
no breath left.

Why do we need so much support to keep on
(you know what I mean; friends) survival
groups, shrinks, spas, tuning, toning, walks,
vacations, vibrations, vitamins, assertive training,
low-fat-non-fat cholesterol-free organic all natural
food (naturally), massage, strokes, pokes, acupuncture,
Chinese herbs, addictions, liposuctions,
possessions, admonitions, transgressions, affairs,
divorces, forms forms forms, reforms, files,
more paper work, past life regressions,
disorders, re-orders, diagnoses, nose jobs,
body shapes, transplants, diets, dyes, funerals,
etcetcetcetc long phone long distance conversations
oh no oh no oh no I don't believe don't believe I

believe #+=
If this is
the price of evolution first thing in the morning

I'm getting down on all 4's
then hum into earth until my 4's
disappear,
(not to mention mind) eat leaves till I shrink
to a tendril and go right
for the sun.

The Writing Group

With joy we sit we cry
we confess we are sorry
we are anxious we are tongue
tied we are heart bound we are
safe we are falling off the cliff of
our heart into a pool of unswum water
so blue we think we are whales we are one
we breach we cry we breathe we burst forth
like a bull through the gate headfirst into the cape
of our lives china splinters silvered translucent under
an eclipsed moon oh watch us jump over mercy leap with
our capes like wings that leave us splendid as never before
we hover on a scarf of air wafted in from somewhere
we have never been but plan to go as soon as possible
yes we are speaking untying our tongues
no longer sorry and then we come down
and go to where we came from but
something is different we are
smiling our minds are blue
and falling and nothing
hurts Amen.

Like A Deer Running

What of Us

What of the baby in the dream too small to hold or diaper?
What of the rattlesnake with fangs and teeth removed
become a little boy's pet?
What of the man in Florida who feeds thousands of pounds
of meat a week to his 3000 alligators while you
who only eat vegetables and fish still find things to snap at.
Later you travel to Florida to attend a family wedding
and read in the newspaper that alligators are almost extinct,
that they will not bite you in Florida or Africa or Australia,
unless you feed them, then you become the meat. And,
you read, everything eats them, including themselves.
What of that.
What of the 13 sea lions washed up together on a stretch
just north of where you live, so badly decomposed
researchers don't know if they were shot or simply all got sick
at once. So your day has pushed against the comfort
of its stretches. So your life didn't quite deliver what you had
in mind. Rumi would say at least you showed up.
It is just as hard to follow one path as another.
My cat knows all about that stretching
from field to tree to patio, dining on lizards and Fancy Feast
all in the same day. What of the chimes that kick in
with no breeze. Somehow the baby will grow, though it may
have to fit into another life. What of the man
who wants to die because he resents no one showed him
his path, not seeing he was always on it. My son
would tell him of terrible things he saw in Costa Rica,
children born on banana plantations between corridors
of hundreds of blue plastic bags that leak, make rivers bite
like snakes, burn children's heads to blimps, arms
that try to walk, legs that pick perfect fruit.
What of the silence of 200,000 my son among them,
200,000 stars bowing to a presence bigger than all of us,
so quiet praying for a miracle, they become one.

The Storytellers

The world is full of us, stories our way of making the world
appear a little less slanted in others' directions, help us gather
some space to nest our being in the largeness of things,
so it wasn't unusual we chose the beach this night
to build a fire fed with odd items we wanted to release
like last year's Christmas tree stand and an antique toilet seat.
It was how easily the fire burned that made me think
of how it was not always so, how a long time ago

in high school the nuns thought I should get some experience
being holy so elected me lighter of the flame for a day,
put a veil on my head, a taper in my hands and pushed me
out on stage before mass to light the candles headed straight
for heaven on the makeshift altar. Nervous with the task,
being a girl and all, not fit to stand before the sacristy,
all I could do was trip and muster, and wouldn't you know
those candles sensed it, felt my insecurity, me fed one thing

having to deliver another. The wicks just turned to mush
at my touch so the padre came stomping to finish the job,
sent me to the wings disgraced while the whole auditorium
of girls burst into giggles burning a hole in my back side.
As I was getting to the moral of my story, how holiness
was not my thing, the toilet seat sputtering with joy,
us rocking under the stars, oil rigs like cartoon monsters
lined up on the horizon and the waves awash with song,

it was then the police wormed in with their lights
to drown us out. We packed up our laughter and
didn't even offer them one marshmallow before
we took off, not one, so when I told the story later
to a friend, who wanted to weave a web safely, she chose
an office to tell her story, lit several votive candles
arranged like the way geese fly, and began by whacking
two stones together. I wondered if anyone ever heard

one rock cry, one grain of sand turn to pearl, and catacombs
came to mind, going underground, and who's free
and no wonder we feel detached from the largeness of things.
In my friend's story a magnificent white owl spread its wings.
As she moved her arms swift above our heads, an owl
appeared on the wall in back of her and no one called
the department of miracles, we just sat there in her spell,
dwelled in her dream of a fawn saving the owl from a rat.

Next morning another friend just arrived home
after living three years in Mexico tells me rats are common
there, and she's getting married again, this time for good.
I am happy for her and give her a crow feather dark as a dream
which reminds her of her ex-father-in-law, an old Chumash,
who told her while they were sitting on top of her roof
that he lost three gold coins when he was a boy
and funny thing, they had never been found,
and because of that he was the richest man alive.

They laughed all day about that, up there on the roof,
laughed the sun down and that's how she will remember him,
how I will remember her, feeling somehow like I finally
got the candle lit, can brush off my backside now and go home
carrying these stories aloft like some torch, carry them
running down the avenue alive with the largeness of things.

The Field Out Back

We bought this house for the field, fooling ourselves
we could be living anywhere, how glance narrowed
to an arrowhead pointing to invaders the other side
of fog, sea filled with echoes whose commands
brought natives running to shore. Somehow
the chain-link fence that separated us from land's spread
meant nothing. The field was ours, the lack
of civilization between scraggled chaparral and weeds,
the sycamores and eucalyptus grove around the creek,
ours to house walk-abouts year by year. The bamboo stand
at the foot of the oak circle was hidden fort of my daughter
and her friend, furnished with recycled car parts and
ship planks, plenty good enough for red-tailed fox
when the girls took off for sleep beneath down. Moist
Sundays between pancakes and paperwork we'd explore
for tracks, even the mountain lion's, whose scream
thinned blood on gold nights. Or, surely the bear
had returned with such longing as ours.

Just after the field was sold a time ago and plowing
began, I came eye to eye with a young coyote and offered it
my grief, but it ran from me as all wild things do,
I the smell of flesh, the enemy who takes and grinds
the earth to death, I who only wants the best for everyone.
I want to hold them all, coyote, fox and lion, the rabbits
darting to the vanished edge. I will be the edge, I call,
will build burrows and caves with extra covers
flung over the collapsed redwood picnic table
under the tangerine tree. I'll string up rope between two
pines and build us a fire tonight, close to the longest one.
Something will be born. We'll teach each other stories
of lives once lived, bless each other's teeth and claws, dine
on elderberries, possess the burning sage, the beat of wind
against earth's skin stretched taut between sea and street.

Just now sun bounces off the red tails of two hawks
who've been with us all along, who still believe
in the field, that they can find the mouse and lift it to
flight, along with our tracks turned under to meet those
gone before. We catch each other like this, the hawks
and I on the patio despite the ploughman who reaches
for his gun, who does not hear me say some things are
too deep to kill.

A Sacred Evening on the Mission Steps Give or Take a Few Flaws

for Louise, who also sings opera

The evening was touted as a sacred one,
a first-time opera event on the Mission steps,
promising holy sounds from a first-rate
symphony and chorus, no mention of
the technician who couldn't make
the musicians budge for a sound check
to balance the speakers despite his pleas
until the handsome first violinist arrived late
and with a sheepish grin rushed them
into plunks and groans, pulling together
the myriad sounds; nothing about an explosion
of canons complete with smoke to capture
the power of Boito we thought were lights
gone bad under faulty wiring. They didn't tell us
high notes might waver in the moist air,
or of the Franciscan monk's unwavering joy
with his dream come true and at intermission
how he would bequeath his divas bouquets
with a rush of grandest gratitude.
Neither publicized were colored lights rayed
against the flat adobe face like God's very smile,
or the pathetic photograph on the program
of an 1840 Chumash Indian orchestra
at this same spot, playing cellos and violins,
their drums and feathers forsaken, rattles
burned perhaps, a monk before them holding
a scroll of music, his hand raised in direction,
yet when we were marched to the inner gardens
for a reception of cultivated hors d'oeuvres,

it was you who saved the night, you humming
soulfully the proper way Verdi's Nabucco
should go which filled me most
as if I had been led into a secret only the blessed
could fathom or the dead could hear,
and the look on your brother's face, too,
yes holy and happier than the monk's,
as your hand waved slowly as in a dirge
which it was you whispered, not *fortissimo,*
your voice, lifted up toward the bells
which didn't, but could have tolled.

Big Fish

I forget too many details thinking
which ones I want to remember
and with each word that refuses
to find its way to my tongue, I worry
I will end up like my father-in-law
whose speech has become Swiss
cheese to our ears. Last night
he pointed out to sea "big fish, big fish"
his arm moving in a great arc
against the silver sky. "They are——
they are——" and in the pause
he jumped his body through the sea
of our eyes, this man who had been unable
to walk these past weeks healing
from back surgery, suddenly leaping
like one of those fish he can't remember
the name of, those fish who don't know
their own names, and there we all are
at sunset leaping with him through
the first brilliance of the foggy day,
leaping, forgetting more and more.

My Son's Fish Tacos

I can live without skunks who run
under the house for cover in the rain
and fires that break your heart, but never
without the satisfaction of salsa,
spreading it over fish tacos my son
taught me to make, and how to slice onions
and garlic without drawing blood
which holds no merit in the seasoning.

In admiration I listen as he points out
the importance of a sharp knife,
how to angle it up at the tip then
a quick press down repeated over and over
like sandpipers scoot after waves drawing back.
I marvel as he chops cilantro, golden squash,
tomatoes, each in their own special stack
for layering on warm tortillas over a bed
of delicately browned white fish,

relish his dexterity in the kitchen
not unlike his maneuvering a wave
balancing platter and presence, delight how
he moves through life as I learn
from him each visit how to hang out,
slice and spice, how to go easy, how
to make the best of what you have.

Where did you learn these things
I ask, wiping my mouth as we feast
on his masterpiece in the same places
where we've always sat through all
the years, counters a tumble and the cat
being a cat wanting out. *Here and there*
he answers knowing that's all I need,
that the pleasure will last months to come.

Like a Deer Running

I get lost inside things, the round of a white O
printed on a book cover become the curve of a wide turn
I made in the fresh snow finally leaning far enough in, bending
the knee deep enough against the slope, the uphill hand parallel,
and then another curve to the right
and everything changed if you "committed,"
as the instructor said, so I went for it
pushing through the crush of my ghosts,
sky and mountain all one sheet like a thought
before form, though usually thought had more texture and shade.

Looking at the O I fall through a tunnel
that goes all the way back to Salem and forward
to the day after tomorrow when I might be even less afraid,
might do anything—what—and think of women
who commit too much, go too far, are sometimes suspended
in mid air, hung—then I began to understand
why it had been hard to get my skis just so if I was fighting
against breaking down like the last time, people yelling
to bend more! and wasn't I—hadn't I always
Bent and bowed as far as possible like some thin tree in the wind?

This time the voice was calm. The instructor tapped
my downhill knee with his pole as if it were a magic wand
and suggested I fold it in, rotate my hip,
something never mentioned before. I did, he said "bingo"
and I took off, imagined making love with the mountain,
and there was this big sigh like a healthy wind
instead of the avalanche-size scream when I broke my leg
hanging between life and death.

As I stood there in the center of the Rockies
where the ski lift dumped me,
the instructor pointed out Holy Cross Mtn. to the west,
said how people once took pilgrimages there for healing
and died in the winter at such altitude
so you shouldn't stake too much on natural phenomena,
like how snow falls in the shape of a cross
or how these mountains were like a necklace for God
as my father had said when I was a child, naming each bead
One by one time after time.

It was something how I was here again but now
looking over these peaks instead of up at them, their names
being spoken again as in a roll call
all saying *here,* my leg finally healed. That didn't mean
I would live to tell about it though at last,
at last I could move with the mountain
a little like a deer running and my father would see
and call out my name
and I would turn like never before—

Fog

I never thought of us living
so close like this, closed as behind a constant scrim that keeps out
everything I want in; trees, moon, stars, sun playing on leaves.
        Only here there is no backlight to bring up the magic
        as on stage when I played the fairy godmother
        100 years ago, or so it seems.
Something about sleeping in this fog, how it lulls you
into thinking paralysis has set in everywhere
and we peer under bushes to see if the prince
is coming to wake us, kiss us free from such doubt
that clings to eyes and clothes, will not wipe clean
from windshields as we make our way to work,
will not wash away with coffee, or how hard we rub our eyes.

        This morning I thought how Sandburg got it wrong
when I let in my cat from a night on the town;
how she thundered in like a bomb! no tiny feet her,
knocking over every loose thing, feathers and flowers
flying everywhere, fog stalking in with her
        into each niche and room,
        each crevice in my head, on the edge of dream
as I tried to remember what I could not remember
except how my sister said she would not visit here again,
never seeing the sun for 7 days.

And so the world unmakes itself here on the coast,
fog an amoeba of ocean,
flesh without bones, nation without boundaries
        that takes and takes everything in its spread
perhaps looking for some direction
with what little time it has to be
a part of something, or perhaps it really means to hide us,
as if by magic, until we decide who we are and light up.

The Wind Nest

Last day of the year a wind blows hot from the mouth of sky
through red hands of poinsettia.
Everything is loose and lifting.
I can't tell the difference between monarchs and leaves,
        wonder how they turn brilliant orange
without frost as I sit on the patio listening to laundry spin.

The sun is too hot to lift my eyes from the page.
Words blow off before they form.
Everything is lifting, everything but this bleakness
                        that matches weather far away.
It should be cold and snowing. I water
wilting sunflowers. Dance around the wind.
            Wind that roars of loss & change & imperfection
            & things not as they should be & as they are
like how I turn my head away from myself and see a nest.
Stiff and soft at once,
intricate weaving and interweaving
of dried grass to form a pouch
broad at the base, thin at the top where it hung from some tree
around here.

                                Once I passed a tree that howled
with no wind around
                        except within its shade.
I stood at its base and listened for a message, my eyes fastened
to its crown.
                                Now I hold this nest
once home for all that was young & innocent & hungry
for height & wide ranges, and finally think the tree
I heard long ago spun its own wind
with nothing to tell me at all.
                                To cast off what needed to fly.
                Besides, it's how they sing themselves to sleep
and some of us are lucky enough to hear.